DRAW

Magical *Fantasies*

A Step-by-Step Guide

Damon J. Reinagle

PEEL productions, inc.

Printed in Hong Kong

Library of Congress Cataloging-in-Publication Data

Reinagle, Damon J.
    Draw Magical fantasies : a step by step guide / Damon J. Reinagle
        p. cm.
    Summary: Provides step-by-step instructions for drawing elves, fairies,
wizards, court jesters, mermaids, and other magical creatures
     ISBN 0-939217-33-3
 1. Fantastic, The, in art--Juvenile literature. 2. Drawing--Technique--
Juvenile literature. [Fairy tales in art. 2. Drawing--Technique.] I. Title.

NC825.F25 R45 2001
741.2--dc21   2001058024

Distributed to the trade and art markets
in North and South America by

NORTH LIGHT BOOKS,
an imprint of F&W Publications, Inc.
4700 East Galbraith Road
Cincinnati, OH 45236

(800) 289-0963

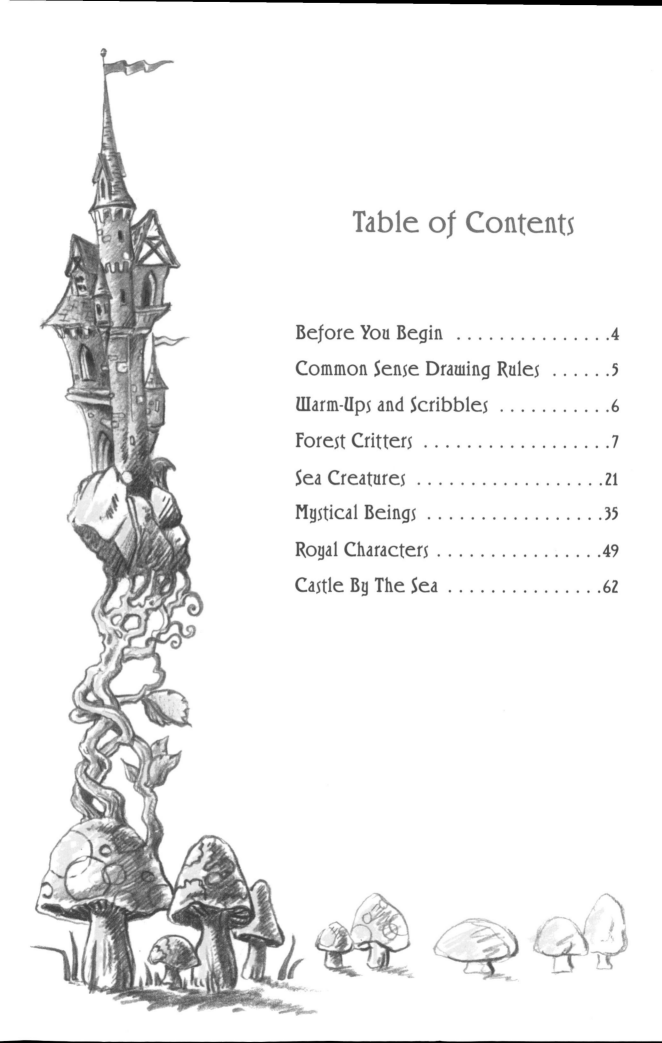

Table of Contents

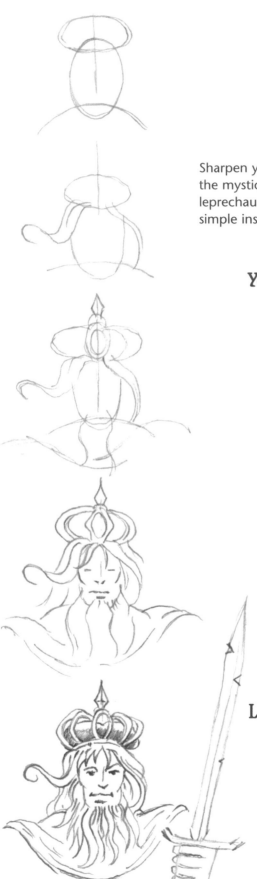

Before You Begin...

Sharpen your imagination as well as your pencil for you're about to enter the mystical land of faeries, elves, mermaids, giants, court jesters, and leprechauns! Draw Magical Fantasies will lead the way, step by step, with simple instructions, common sense drawing rules, and basic shapes.

You will need:

- a pencil
- a pencil sharpener
- an eraser
- paper
- a ruler
- a place to draw
- colored pencils
- a SUPER POSITIVE ATTITUDE!
- and, a belief in MAGIC!

(I Do Believe!)

Let the magical drawing adventures begin!

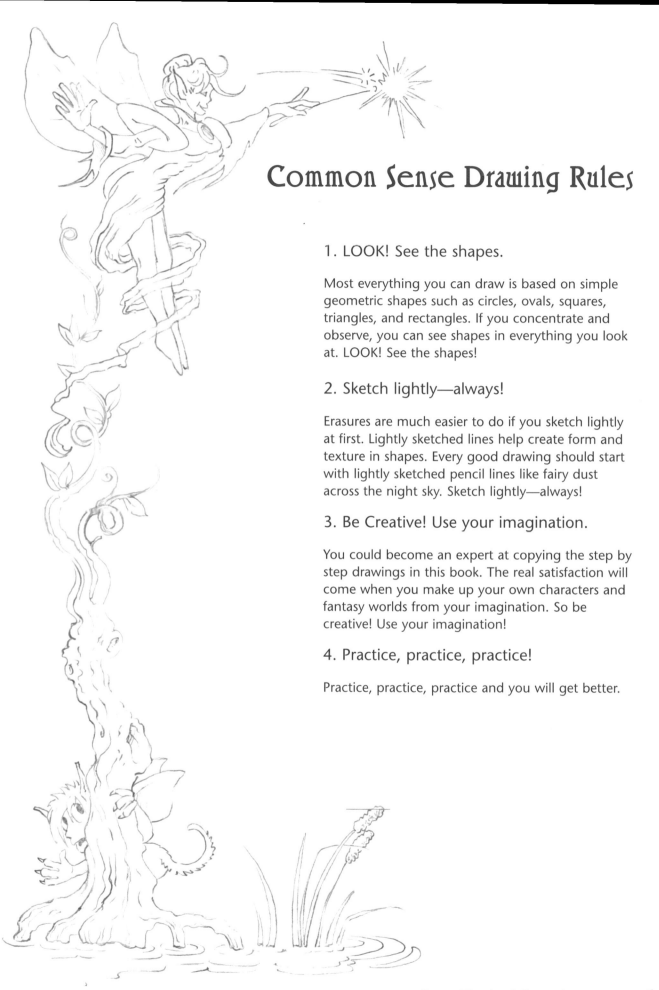

Common Sense Drawing Rules

1. LOOK! See the shapes.

Most everything you can draw is based on simple geometric shapes such as circles, ovals, squares, triangles, and rectangles. If you concentrate and observe, you can see shapes in everything you look at. LOOK! See the shapes!

2. Sketch lightly—always!

Erasures are much easier to do if you sketch lightly at first. Lightly sketched lines help create form and texture in shapes. Every good drawing should start with lightly sketched pencil lines like fairy dust across the night sky. Sketch lightly—always!

3. Be Creative! Use your imagination.

You could become an expert at copying the step by step drawings in this book. The real satisfaction will come when you make up your own characters and fantasy worlds from your imagination. So be creative! Use your imagination!

4. Practice, practice, practice!

Practice, practice, practice and you will get better.

Warm-Ups and Scribbles

Warm-ups and scribbles loosen your hand and your imagination.

Take some scrap paper and practice drawing circles. Barely let your pencil touch the paper as you lightly sketch circles over and over again.

Practice warm-ups and scribbles with straight lines, wavy lines, jagged and wiggly lines.

Develop the unique artist's touch by practicing warm-ups and scribbles with circles and lines every day.

Practice, practice, practice and you will get better.

LOOK!

See the Shapes!

Can you see the ovals, circles, squares, triangles, and rectangles in these drawings?

Almost all the figures in this book begin with oval-shaped heads.

The bodies of the figures are drawn with basic shapes too—circles, ovals, rectangles, and triangles.

Arms and legs sometimes begin as ovals or as lines (rods) and circles (joints) to help you envision the direction and proportion.

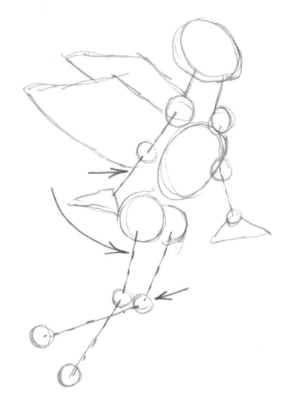

The Troll

This dwarf lives in the rocks under the drawbridge.

1 Lightly sketch a circle for the head and a circle for the body. Sketch three stacked ovals for his left and right leg.

2 Sketch two circles for his eyes. Sketch three connecting ovals for his right arm and hand. Sketch four connecting ovals for his left arm and hand.

3 Sketch a long cone shape for his club. Sketch four small ovals for his big nose. Draw two curved lines for his tattered overall strap. Erase extra sketch lines.

4 Starting at the top, draw his head, ears, and eyes. Put a wart on his nose. Draw his jagged shirt sleeves and his arms. Add patches to his overalls.

5 LOOK carefully at the final drawing! Add the details you see. Don't forget his dark eyes, fang teeth, and warts galore.

   Shade and color this ugly character.

ARTIST'S TIP:

See how many body parts can be started as lightly sketched circles and ovals. Just erase the extra sketch lines later!

The Giant

With a mere stomp of his foot, this giant can make the earth quake and mountains tumble. You can draw this club swinger in five easy steps. So, fee-fi-fo, ready? GO!

1 Sketch an oval for the head. Sketch two circles for the shoulders. Draw an arching line, from the head to the left shoulder.

2 Draw three curved lines— one for the chest, one for the stomach, and one for the bottom of his BIG belly!

3 Draw one curly hair line. LOOK at his face! Draw the curved lines for his eyes, cheeks, nostrils, and mouth.

Using the rod (line) and joint (circle) system, sketch lines and circles for his right hand. Sketch his left arm and hand.

Draw large ovals for his thick thighs and circles for his round knees. Draw lines for his legs. Sketch the shapes you see to begin his feet.

On the ground, sketch two small ovals to begin drawing his archenemy.

4 Add the mouth line. Draw
   his left shoulder, arm, hand,
   and fingers. Draw his right
   arm, hand, and curved
   fingers. Draw his club.

   Draw curved lines below his
   knees for boot tops. Add
   lines to shape his boots.
   Erase extra sketch lines.

   Draw legs and a tail on the
   mouse.

5 Look carefully at the final
   drawing! Starting at the top,
   add hair, more face lines,
   teeth, and all the details you
   see—head to toe.

   Shade and color.

   Don't forget the fierce
   rodent. Add its whiskers,
   ears, and eye.

ARTIST'S TIP:

LOOK! See the simple shadow
under the mouse and giant?
Shadows always make things
seem more alive!

The Elf

Ever wonder what the mischievous elves do all day? I caught this elf just hanging out in the forest, playing pool!

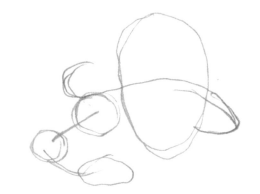

1   Sketch an oval for the head. Sketch a curved "S" shape to begin his hat. Using the rod (line) and joint (circle) system, sketch lines and circles for his right arm and hand.

2   Add long curved lines for his hat. Draw his right arm. Add a curved line for his shirt. Draw his belt. Sketch the skirt shape.

Sketch a line and a circle for his left arm and hand. Draw four short lines to begin his outstretched fingers.

3   Erase extra lines. Draw his pointy right ear. Add a curved line, behind the ear, for his hat. Draw his right arm sleeve. Add finger lines. Draw his left hand.

Using the rod (line) and joint (circle) system, sketch lines and circles for his legs and feet.

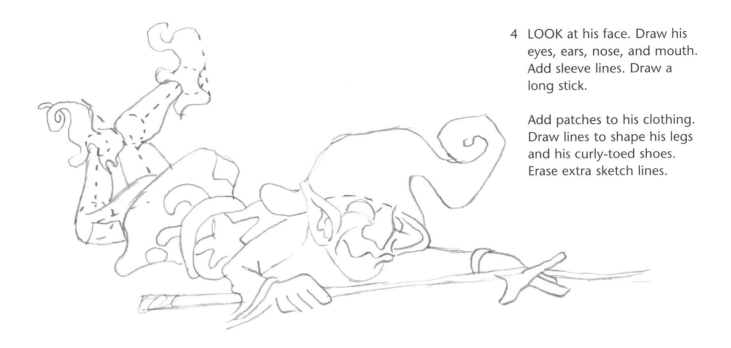

4 LOOK at his face. Draw his eyes, ears, nose, and mouth. Add sleeve lines. Draw a long stick.

Add patches to his clothing. Draw lines to shape his legs and his curly-toed shoes. Erase extra sketch lines.

ARTIST'S TIP:

Figures in action are always more interesting than ones that just stand there! When you create characters, show them in action. This elf loves to shoot pool.

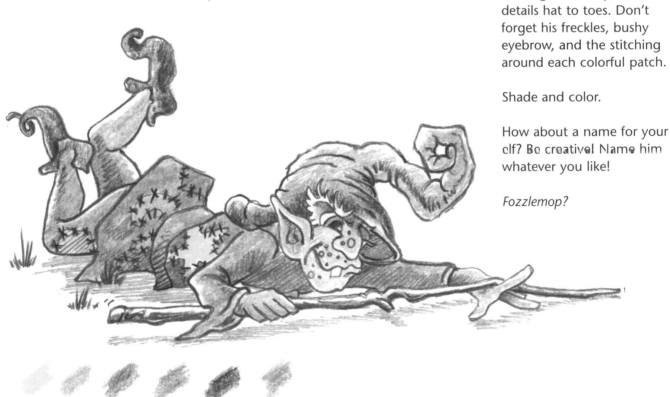

5 LOOK at the final drawing! Starting at the top, add details hat to toes. Don't forget his freckles, bushy eyebrow, and the stitching around each colorful patch.

Shade and color.

How about a name for your elf? Be creative! Name him whatever you like!

Fozzlemop?

The Fairy Godmother

How would you like to have a fairy godmother to grant your every wish? Here is your chance to create your very own.

1 Sketch a circle and an oval for her head. Draw one curly strand of hair. Draw three curved lines for her collar.

2 Draw more hair lines, on top of her head.

LOOK carefully at her wide shoulders and outstretched arms. Draw the ovals and triangles you see. Sketch the connecting rods (lines) and joints (circles) for her left arm and hand. Sketch a fan shape for the fingers.

3 Draw more hair lines. LOOK carefully at her profile! Draw it. Add her pointed ear.

Draw her right wrist and hand. Sketch her upper body and hips.

Sketch her butterfly wings.

4 LOOK at the markings on the wings! Add these. Add a finger on her right hand. Draw her left hand and fingers.

Sketch the connecting rods (lines) and joints (circles) for her legs and feet. Draw curving lines for her swirling dress.

5 LOOK at the final drawing! Draw her legs, feet, and pointed toes. Erase extra lines. Draw all the details you see. Don't forget her magical wand and eyeglasses. Add more swirling cloth lines to make her look like she's floating on air.

Shade and color.

Groovy godmother!

Now make a wish!

The Faerie Dragon

This flying lizard, small enough to carry in your pocket, is a gentle creature who lives deep in the woods.

1 Draw two small circles for the dragon's eyes. Sketch a circle for the cheek. Draw a curved line for her long chin. Draw two curved lines for her lovely neck.

2 Draw one wild, curly strand of hair. Add a small curved line to connect the eyes. Add eyelids. Draw her bumpy nose. Add another curved line to shape her neck.

Sketch connecting rods (lines) and joints (ovals) to begin her arms.

3 Add more hair lines. Sketch her triangular ear. Sketch two lines, back from her jaw. Add a nose line. Draw the mouth. Draw lines to shape her arms and hands. Draw a circle for her crystal ball.

Starting at the back neck line, draw a long curved line for her back and curled tail. Add belly lines. Draw a large oval for her hip. Draw two horizontal ovals, side by side, to begin her lower legs. Add two curved lines for her feet.

4 Add the antennae. Draw the ear ridges. Sketch the wings. Draw a star on her crystal ball. Add claws to her left hand. Draw fingers and claws on her right hand. Draw lines for scales on her neck and belly.

Draw her legs and feet. Draw another curved line to form her thick tail. Erase extra sketch lines.

5 LOOK carefully at the final drawing! Add details you see. Don't forget her eyelashes.

Shade and color.

Dynamite dragon!

ARTIST'S TIP:

Create depth by shading the back leg and arm.

Flying Faerie

Deep in the forest, kindness is always rewarded. But, when anything threatens this peaceful community, you can count on the fairies to unite, sound the alarm, and defend their forest home.

1   Sketch an oval for the head. Sketch two small ovals, below it, to begin the body.

2   LOOK at the girl's profile. Draw it. Add a triangular eye. Draw long, flowing hair lines. Using rods (lines) and joints (circles), sketch the outreaching arm.

3   Draw lines to shape the arm and hand. Draw more flowing lines for hair. Draw a line to connect the breast oval with her rib cage and tummy. Using rods (lines) and joints (circles), sketch her legs.

4   Draw lines to shape her legs and feet. Erase extra sketch lines. Add more flowing hair lines.

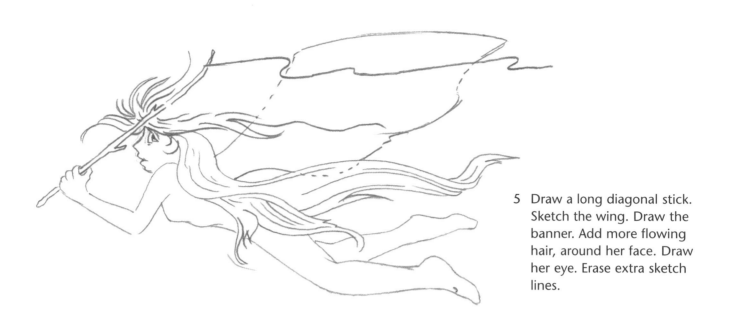

5 Draw a long diagonal stick. Sketch the wing. Draw the banner. Add more flowing hair, around her face. Draw her eye. Erase extra sketch lines.

6 LOOK carefully at the final drawing! Add details. Write any message you wish on the banner. Don't forget the stars and bubbles.

Shade and color.

LOOK! See the shapes!

The heads of these fanciful characters are drawn almost entirely from basic geometric shapes. When you add details you can create a magical drawing. Give these a try—one step at a time. Use your imagination to create *your own* unique design.

Chapter 2 - Sea Creatures

The Mermaid

One of the most legendary and elusive of all fairy tale characters is the mermaid. With the upper body of a woman and the tail of a fish, she's quick! Better start sketching before she disappears.

1   Sketch a tilted oval for her head. Note the angle. Draw a curved line for her neck. Sketch another tilted oval for her torso. Draw a long curved line for her tail.

2   Draw her profile on the right side of the head oval. Add a circle to the top of her head for a sand dollar barrette. Sketch two circles for her breasts. Erase extra lines.

    From the bottom of the torso, draw a second connecting, curved line to form her tail. Sketch tail flippers.

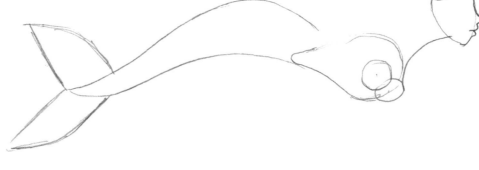

3   Starting at the top of her head, draw long flowing hair lines. Draw a small triangle for her eye. Using rods (lines) and joints (circles), sketch her arms. Add lines to the tail flippers.

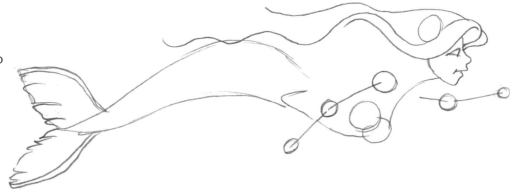

4 Draw more flowing hair lines. Add lines to shape her arms and hands. Draw seashells over her breasts. Erase extra lines.

5 LOOK carefully at the final drawing! Add details you see. Don't forget her eyelashes and fingers.

Shade and color.

(For instructions on drawing the fish, see page 32.)

The Merman

Even more elusive than the mermaid is the king of the ocean, the merman.

1 Sketch an oval for his head, an oval for his torso, and a circle for his stomach.

2 Starting at the top of his head, draw flowing hair lines. Draw lines to begin his moustache.

Sketch ovals for his shoulders. Draw lines for his chest and rib cage.

3 Add more hair lines. Draw his moustache. Draw abdominal muscles. Sketch two more ovals for each arm.

Draw the hips. LOOK carefully at the angle of his tail and flippers. Sketch these shapes.

4   Starting at the top, draw the eyes. Draw the beard. Add lines to shape his muscular shoulders, arms, and hands. Add his belly button. Draw "V" shape scales on his hips. Draw curved lines to shape his tail and flippers. Draw two straight lines to begin his spear. Erase extra sketch lines.

5   LOOK at the final drawing! Add details. Add a three-tipped trident to his spear. Don't forget his gold bracelet. How about some seaweed?

Shade and color.

ARTIST'S TIP:

Long flowing hair creates a water current illusion. Shading adds realism.

Sitting Mermaid

Under the sea, she sits and waits—hoping her true love will return someday. Until then she'll sit, and splash, and play.

1   Sketch a tilted oval for her head. Sketch a triangle for her neck. Sketch circles for her shoulders.

2   Using rods (lines) and joints (circles), sketch her left arm. Draw her breasts. Sketch a circle for the rib cage. Draw her right arm. Draw lines for her hips and long tail.

3   Add hair lines. Draw lines to shape the left arm and hand.

   Sketch the rectangular shaped rock. Under the rock, sketch her tail flipper.

4 Draw a starfish in her hair. Add more flowing hair lines. Draw her face. Add the ear. Draw shells on her breasts. Add a strap. Draw a thumb on her left hand.

Draw lines to form diamond shaped scales, on her tail. Draw the rock. Add additional rocks beneath. Erase extra lines.

5 LOOK at the final drawing! Head to tail, add the details you see.

Shade and color.

(See Seahorse drawing instructions on page 32.)

Magnificent mermaid!

The Pirate Queen

Most Pirates ye be hearin 'bout are sea farin' men, but this lass is also a gritty sailor! Don't be fooled by her golden hair and eyes so blue, er she is as fierce a pirate as I ever knew!

1 Sketch an oval for her head. Sketch two small ovals, wide apart, for her broad shoulders.

2 Add hair lines. Sketch a triangle shape for her coat collar.

3 Add more lines for hair. Draw the torso. Draw ruffles for her blouse.

4 LOOK at her fancy hat! Draw the hat. Add more hair. Using rods (lines) and joints (circles), sketch her arms and hands.

   Draw her belt and buckle. Sketch her coat.

5 Starting at the top, add a line for her hat trim. Draw a circle and a long curved line to begin the feather. Draw the eyes, nose, and lip. Draw lines to shape her arms, hands, and fingers. Sketch wrist cuffs.

Draw the sword. Add the pistol.

Sketch ovals for her legs. Add a pant line and coat lines. Sketch the boots. Erase extra sketch lines.

6 LOOK at the final drawing! Hat to boots, add the details you see. Don't forget the coat trim and the fancy epaulets on the shoulders.

Shade and color.

Draw Magical Fantasies   29

Sea Serpent

Deep down, at the bottom of the sea, this scaly serpent devours the remains of a sunken ship. Best to steer clear o' this beast, 'less ye be his next meal!

1 Sketch an oval, with a line down the middle. Sketch a triangle, overlapping the oval, for the face. Sketch an oval for the body. Draw a curved line on his chest. Add a line to separate his pectorals.

2 LOOK at the shape of his head! Draw it. Add the eyes, nose, and mouth. Draw curved lines for his round shoulders and biceps. Sketch his left hand. Draw four curved lines, under his chest, to begin his abdominal muscles.

3 Add horns, ears, and hair. Add lines to shape his face. Draw nostrils. Draw his beard. Add lines to outline his muscular shoulders.

Erase extra lines. Sketch fingers on his left hand. Add more abdominal muscles. Draw the serratus muscles on his sides. Draw his long curving tail.

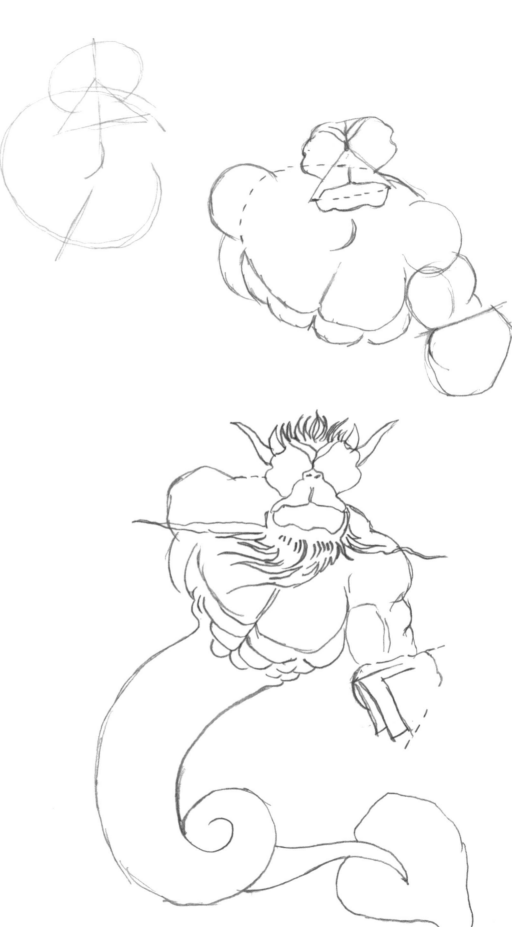

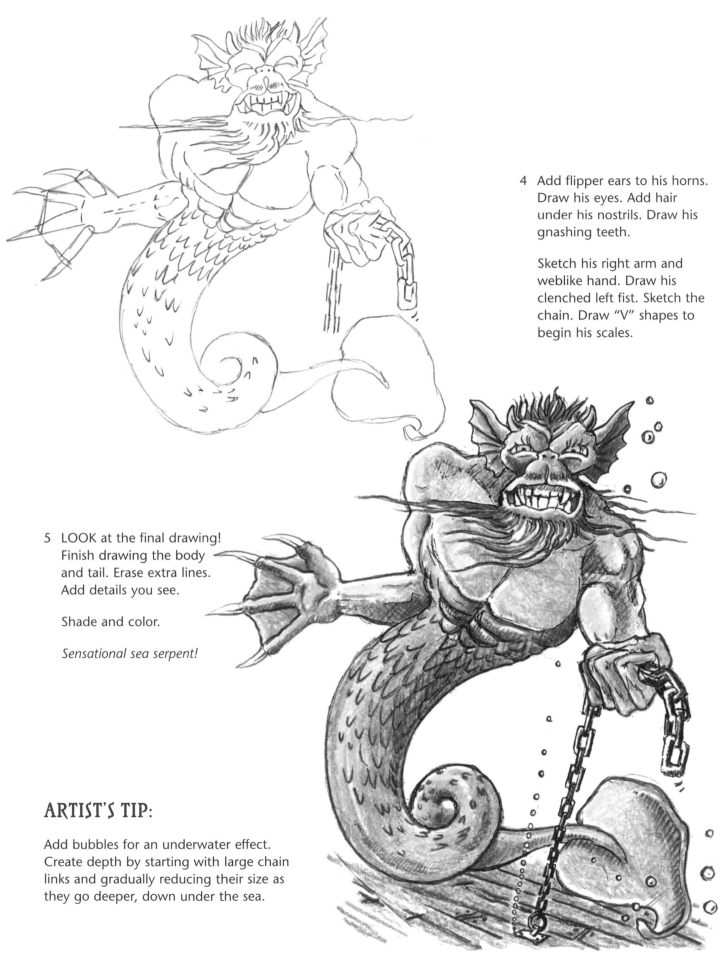

4 Add flipper ears to his horns. Draw his eyes. Add hair under his nostrils. Draw his gnashing teeth.

Sketch his right arm and weblike hand. Draw his clenched left fist. Sketch the chain. Draw "V" shapes to begin his scales.

5 LOOK at the final drawing! Finish drawing the body and tail. Erase extra lines. Add details you see.

Shade and color.

Sensational sea serpent!

ARTIST'S TIP:

Add bubbles for an underwater effect. Create depth by starting with large chain links and gradually reducing their size as they go deeper, down under the sea.

Sea Life

The sea is full of colorful creatures of all shapes and sizes.

LOOK at the seahorse! What shapes do you see?

1. Sketch a circle for the head and one for the eye. Sketch the mouth. Draw curved lines for the body and tail.

2. Add a circle to the eye. Draw triangle shapes on his spine for fins. Add squiggly lines on his underside. Lightly sketch his dorsal fin.

3. LOOK at the final drawing! Erase extra lines. Add details you see.

   Shade and color.

LOOK at the fish! What shapes do you see?

1. Sketch an oval for the head. Add a circle for the eye. Sketch the body oval. Sketch a half-circle to begin the tail.

2. Sketch the triangular mouth. Add a circle to the eye. Sketch the fins.

3. LOOK at the final drawing! Erase extra lines. Add details you see.

   Shade and color.

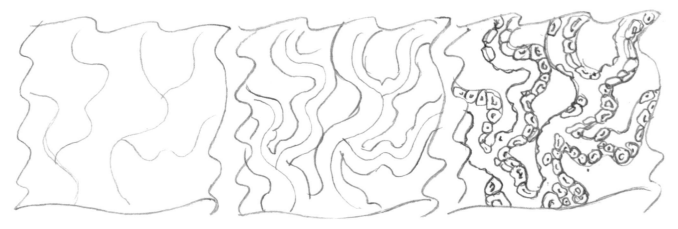

Coral:

To begin, sketch a box shape with wavy lines. Sketch more wavy lines inside the box. Add more wavy lines, inside and outside the original lines. Draw lots of small oval shapes inside the lines to form the coral. Add shading and color.

Undersea Scene:

Sections A and E are the lightly sketched beginnings of an undersea scene. Parts B and D show more details added. Section C shows the finished drawing with more details and shading. See the contrast of light and dark in the middle section.

The Magical Frog

*Frogs aren't exactly sea farin'
amphibians but this guy was
discovered, alive and hopping, in
the sunken treasure chest.*

1 Sketch an oval, to begin his
   crown. Sketch a circle for his
   eye and an oval for his head.
   Look at the body lines and
   ovals! Sketch these. Sketch
   two lines beneath him for a
   branch to perch on.

2 Sketch 5 small circles atop
   his crown. Sketch "V"
   shapes inside the oval. Draw
   a circle around his right eye
   and a half circle for his left
   eye. Draw his mouth. Draw
   lines to shape his arms, legs,
   fingers, and toes.

3 LOOK carefully at the final
   drawing! Go over sketch
   lines to better shape the
   frog. Erase extra lines. Add
   the details you see. Draw
   small circles all over his
   head, legs, and arms to give
   him a lumpy look.

   Shade and color.

RIBBIT!!! Fun frog!

Chapter 4 - Mystical Beings

The Leprechaun

Best to stay on the good side of this mischievous character. He often grants wishes but he has also been known to play a trick or two.

1 Sketch an oval for his head. Draw a boomerang shape for his hat brim. Draw the hat top.

2 Draw a large "U" shaped mouth. Erase extra sketch lines. Sketch his body. Add lines for his vest.

3 Draw a line for the hat band. Sketch a wide "V" shaped cape across his shoulders. Sketch lines and ovals to shape his left arm and hand. Sketch lines to shape his right arm and hand.

Sketch his legs and feet. Sketch his long walking stick.

4 Starting at the top, add stars and a shamrock to his hat. Sketch his pointed ears. Draw his eyes, nose, and mouth. Go over the cape lines to make folds. Add an oval for his jeweled broach.

Draw lines to form fingers on his left hand. Go over the walking stick to make it more realistic.

Add lines to shape the right hand and fingers. Add lines on the vest for the armhole and patches. Sketch his leather bag.

5 LOOK at the final drawing! Add the details you see. Don't forget his big white teeth and his chubby feet. Add a wee bit more magic with dots and sparkles swirling around his walking stick.

Shade and color.

Lively leprechaun!

The Wizard Poulter

Any royal court worthy of its kingdom wouldn't make a move without consulting its resident psychic, the wizard! This guy can cast spells and performs a really cool trick with pebbles and snakes.

1 Sketch a tilted oval for the head. Sketch the shapes you see for the wizard's hat.

2 Draw lines to shape the hat. Draw his profile. Draw lines for his long flowing beard. Erase extra sketch lines.

3 Draw more beard and hair lines. Add a moustache.

   Using rods (lines) and joints (circles), sketch his arms and hands. Sketch the top of his robe.

4 LOOK carefully at this drawing! Draw his right hand and fingers. Sketch his power stick with a large "S" shape on top. Sketch his rectangular right sleeve. Sketch lines for the chains he wears.

   Starting at the top, draw stars and crescent moon shapes on his hat and robe.

5. Sketch a belt with a buckle. Draw a circle for a potion bag.

   Sketch the long, flowing robe bottom. Decorate it with stars, moons, and planets. Draw his feet and sandal straps.

6 LOOK at the final drawing! Add the details you see. Don't forget his beads, his cross, and his belt holes.

   Shade and color.

ARTIST'S TIP:

Use your imagination! This wizard is on a cliff. Place yours floating on a cloud or on top of a castle.

The Angel

Angels have been messenger of good tidings through the ages. This angel carries a sword to symbolize strength and justice. She also carries a cross to symbolize faith.

1   Sketch a tilted oval for the head. Draw a "U" shape for her dress neck line. Sketch her left shoulder. Sketch her right sleeve.

2   Draw over the head oval to shape her right cheek and chin. Draw squiggly lines for her sleeves. Draw a line for her back. Sketch lines for her breasts. Sketch an oval for her rib cage.

3   Using rods (lines) and joints (circles), sketch her arms and hands. Sketch a cross in her right hand.

    Draw lines for her waist and hips. Sketch an oval for her thigh.

4   Starting at the top, add curly hair lines. Draw her eyes, nose and mouth. Sketch lines to begin her wings.

    Draw lines to shape her arms and fingers. Add lines to shape the cross

5 LOOK at the wings! Sketch the missing sections. Add curved lines to divide the right wing into five parts. Draw feathers.

Using rods (lines) and joints (circles), sketch her legs. Sketch her feet. Draw lines to shape her right thigh and legs. Erase sketch lines

6 LOOK at the final drawing! Starting at the top, draw the halo. Add the details you see. Don't forget her long eyelashes and flowing dress.

Shade and color.

Awesome angel!

ARTIST'S TIP:

Don't compare my drawing to yours. Just do your best! Make your drawing uniquely yours!

The Lantern Fairy

Early in the wee hours of dawn, when most are still asleep, the lantern faeries go a flyn', lightin' the way for the glistening dew.

1 LOOK at the curves in this drawing! Sketch a tilted oval for the head. Draw two long hair lines on her right side. Using rods (lines) and joints (circles), sketch her left arm and hand. Draw one short hair line from the head to the shoulder circle. Draw one really long, flowing hair line down across the face.

2 Starting at the top, sketch her tiara. Sketch her eyes, nose, and mouth. Using rods (lines) and joints (circles), sketch her right arm and hand. Draw three straight lines to begin the lantern.

Sketch a triangle to begin her wing. Draw lines to shape her left arm. Add a square to begin her fingers. Draw a long oval for her thigh. Draw an oval for her calf. Sketch a circle and an oval to begin her left foot.

Draw another really long hair line flowing from her head across her shoulder, under her arm, and down her thigh crossing beneath her knee.

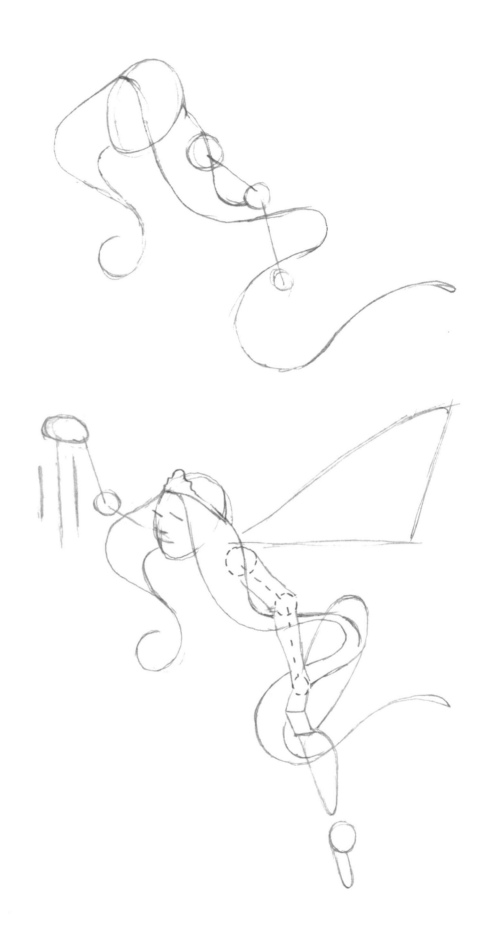

3 Look carefully at the wings!
   Draw them. Draw the eyes,
   eyelashes, nose, and mouth.
   Draw lines to shape the
   right arm, hand, and fingers.
   Add hair lines. Draw the
   lantern. Erase extra sketch
   lines.

   Using rods (lines) and joints
   (circles), sketch her right leg.

4 LOOK at the final drawing!
   Add the details you see.
   Don't forget her designer
   wings.

   Shade and color.

The Magical Unicorn

Nothing is more mystical than the elusive unicorn! Its horn is believed to carry great powers and, therefore is a prize for any evil poacher who would steal it from the great steed!

1   Draw a circle and a "U" shape for the head. Sketch an oval for the neck.

2   Sketch two overlapping circles for the unicorn's shoulders. Sketch a curved line to shape the back, thigh, and belly.

3   Starting at the top, draw a triangle for the ear. Draw the long, flowing mane. Draw a triangle for the eye. Sketch a circle and an upside-down "U" to begin the mouth.

    LOOK carefully at the angle of the legs! Using rods (lines) and joints (circles), sketch the unicorn's four legs.

4 Draw a long, triangle for a horn. Add more flowing lines for the mane on the head and down the neck.

Draw lines to shape the legs. Erase extra sketch lines. Draw curved lines to begin the tail.

5 LOOK at the final drawing! STOP! Sharpen your pencil! Add the details you see. Don't forget the goatee and the flowers.

Shade and color. Add a simple shadow.

Unique unicorn!

Draw Magical Fantasies   **45**

Genie

A genie is a spirit who obeys the person who summons it and always grants the person's wishes.

1. Sketch a tilted oval for the head. Sketch a rounded square shape for the upper body.

2. Sketch a triangle to begin the ear. Sketch lines for the collar and lapels. Sketch two overlapping circles for his right shoulder and upper arm. Sketch a large oval for his body.

3. Starting at the top, draw lines to shape his pointed ear. Add lines to form the large collar. Draw his right sleeve.

   Draw lines and an oval to shape his right arm. Sketch the hand shape and a round shape to begin the energy blast from his hand. Draw lines from the body to shape his swirling tail.

   Sketch ovals and a line to begin the Genie lamp.

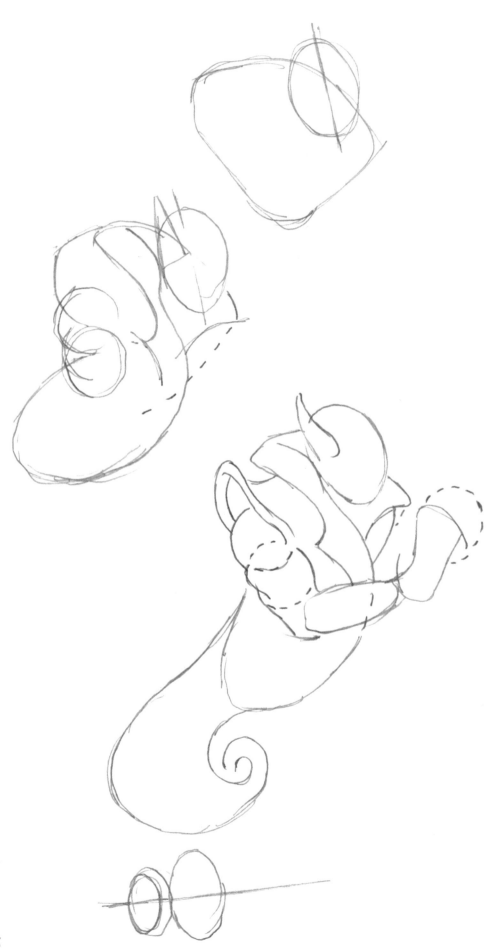

4 Starting at the top, draw one long curly hair. Draw his profile. Add ear lines. Add lines to make his arm more muscular. Draw his hand and fingers. Draw spiked, jagged lines to form the blast. Sketch the shapes you see to begin his left arm and hand.

Draw more swirling lines for his tail. Draw lines to shape the lamp.

5 LOOK at the final drawing! Add all the details you see. Don't forget the moon and stars on his clothing.

Shade and color! Add a shadow under the lamp.

Beast or Beauty?

You've heard that beauty is in the eye of the beholder. As the artist, you decide!

1 Sketch six ovals and a line to begin this face.

2 Sketch two curved lines for the top of the head. Add two curved lines around each eye. Draw two more curved lines on each side to begin the nose.

3 Draw the horns. LOOK at the ears. Draw these. Add lines to shape the nose. Sketch the beard and mouth.

4 LOOK at the final drawing! Add the details you see.

Shade and color.

Chapter 3 - Royal Characters

The Prince

This noble prince is enjoying a favorite royal sport—training his falcon to hunt for game.

1   Sketch an oval for his head. Sketch a long "V" shape for his neck. Sketch a curved line for his shoulders. Draw two curved lines to begin the collar of his cape.

2   Draw two more curved lines for the cape. Sketch three straight lines for his upper body.

3   Draw a slim headband. Draw eyes, nose, and a mouth. Sketch lines for his sweeping cape. Sketch dashed lines over his chest. Using rods (lines) and joints (circles), sketch his arms. Above his extended left arm, sketch a long oval shape to begin the falcon.

Draw lines for his belt and belt buckle. Sketch lines for his squarish skirt. Using rods (lines) and joints (circles), sketch his legs and feet.

4 Starting at the top, add hair. Draw eyebrows, nose, and mouth. Add an ear. Draw lines to shape the cape. Draw his glove. Sketch ovals and wings on the falcon.

Sketch the front of the cape. Draw the round cinch. Draw lines to shape his right arm. Draw his sword. Draw a small square within the belt buckle.

Draw lines to shape his legs and boots. Erase extra sketch lines.

5 LOOK at the final drawing! Add all the details you see. Don't forget the falcon's feathers and the details on the prince's sword. (See page 49 for color ideas.)

Playful prince!

ARTIST'S TIP:

Clean up! Erase any smudges. Notice how a little shading, under his boot fringe and under his belt, adds depth to the drawing.

Draw Magical Fantasies   51

The Princess Warrior

While the prince is out hunting with his falcon, this princess is after other game! Armed with a crystal laser staff, (hey, this is a fantasy, right?) she's ready to take on any intruders that might threaten her kingdom!

1   Sketch a slightly tilted oval, for the head. Draw the neck line and shoulder lines.

2   Draw hair lines. Add shoulder pad lines and two curved lines under her neck.

3   Add more hair. Draw the breastplate vest. Draw her necklace. Add a triangle for a belt buckle.

4   Using rods (lines) and joints (circles), sketch her arms and hands. Sketch ovals for her thighs and calves. Using rods (lines) and joints (circles), sketch her feet. Draw a skirt.

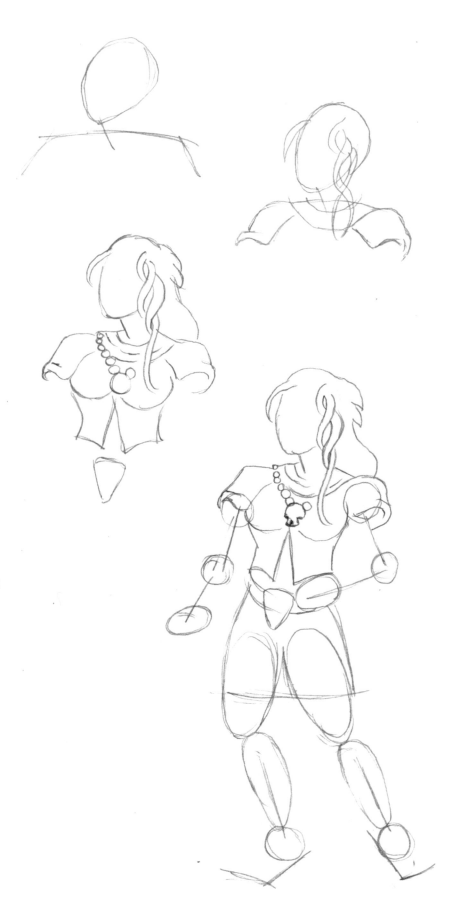

5 LOOK ! See the details? Starting at the top, draw more hair. Add the eyes, nose, and mouth lines. Draw lines to shape her arms and gloves.

Sketch her crystal laser staff. Add lines to the crystal for sparkles. Draw the cape. Draw the jagged skirt bottom. Draw her legs and boots. Erase extra lines.

6 LOOK at the final drawing! Add more hair lines. Draw the flower and leaves headband. Add all the details you see. Don't forget her pleated skirt and the fur on her boots.

Shade and color.

Powerful princess!

The Queen of Hearts

Her majesty, the Queen of Hearts, was a ruthless croquet player in Alice's Wonderland. Our queen doesn't play croquet, but she is an intriguing and colorful dresser.

1   Sketch an oval for her head. Sketch a curved line for her shoulders. Draw two straight lines for the neck and hair. Sketch the square neckline of her dress.

2   Draw a small bun. Add a curved hair line. Draw over the head oval to indent a space for her eye. Add another line for the square neckline. Sketch an oval and circles for her necklace. Draw a long, straight hair line.

3   Sketch her crown. Draw more hair lines. Sketch lines for her sleeves and the bodice (top) of her dress. Using rods (lines) and Joints (circles), sketch her arms and hands.

4   Add five small circles to her crown. Draw her facial features. Add a curved line to begin her cape collar. Add a circle to her necklace. Draw lines to shape her arms and hands. Sketch her muff over her right arm. Draw a straight line under each arm. Sketch the skirt and the cross-ties from her waist.

5 LOOK at the queen, crown to toe! Detail her crown. Draw pearls on her bun. Draw braids. Go over her facial features. Draw the rest of the collar. Make wrinkles for the furry muff.

Draw her wand. Draw the skirt of her gown. Add fur trim along the bottom.

6 LOOK at the final drawing! Add all the details you see. Don't forget the crown on her staff and the hearts on her gown.

Shade and color.

Lovely queen!

His Royal Majesty

Strong, confident and handsome, this king is feared by his enemies and loved by the subjects he rules and protects.

1 Sketch a horizontal oval for a crown. Sketch an oval for the head. Sketch an arch to begin his neck and shoulders.

2 Sketch lines for hair, on each side of his head. Sketch a curved line to begin his cape.

3 Add jewels to his crown. Add more lines for hair and beard. Draw the cape front. Sketch a chain with hanging charms. Sketch a pocket shape to begin his right hand.

4 Draw finger lines and a sword handle, above and below the clenched hand. Sketch the arm oval. Sketch two ovals and a triangle for his left arm and hand. Draw his vest. Sketch long rectangles for his thighs. Sketch his boots.

5 Starting at the top, draw his crown. Draw his eyes, nose, and mouth. Add more beard lines. Add lines to shape his left arm and glove. Draw his flowing cape. Sketch a line for the sword.

6 LOOK at the final drawing! Add details you see. Don't forget the wrinkles on his pants.

Shade and color.

Mighty king!

Draw Magical Fantasies   **57**

The Court Jester

Nothing livens up the cold stone castle like the clowning around of a bumbling royal jester!

1 Sketch an oval for the head. Draw curved lines across his forehead to begin the hat. Sketch a curved line with ovals at each end, for shoulders and arms.

2 Draw two "U" shapes to begin his shirt. Sketch lines for his long left sleeve. Draw a small oval at the end.

3 Sketch a circle and curved lines for a hand and fingers. Draw over his shirt sleeve to make it flow.

Sketch the shape of his skirt. Sketch ovals for his thighs. Using rods (lines) and joints (circles), sketch his legs.

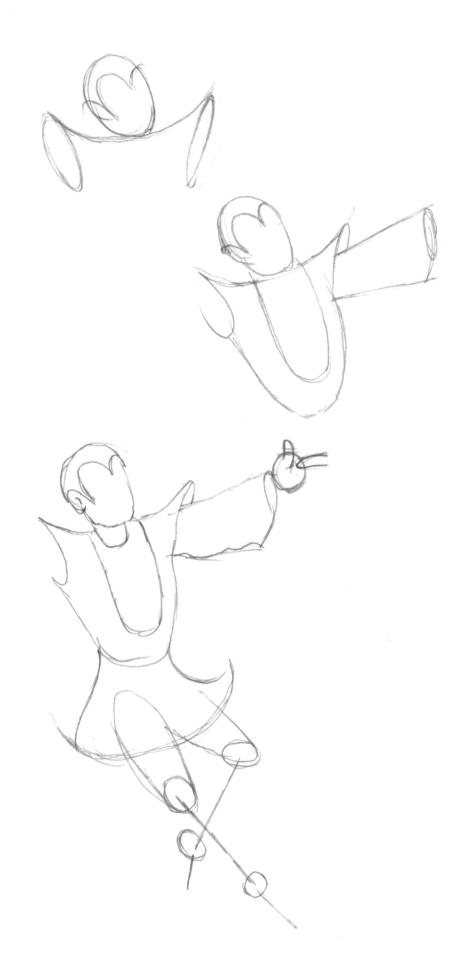

4 Draw the three sections of the jester hat. Add an ear. Draw his facial features. Draw his right sleeve and hand. Draw lines, circles, and diamonds to shape the Jingling Johnny stick.

Draw curved lines with circles at the end for his skirt. Draw lines to shape his legs and feet. Erase extra lines.

5 LOOK at the final drawing! Add all the details you see. Draw bells and cymbals on the Jingling Johnny stick. Draw stripes and polka dots. Shade and color.

Jolly jester!

ARTIST'S TIP:

A variety of patterns on clothing add excitement and contrast to the overall look of a character.

A Royal Scene

When you place characters together in a picture, you can add interest by overlapping them. LOOK carefully at this royal court scene! Notice how the princess covers up part of the king and the jester. Overlapping adds convincing depth to a drawing.

LOOK at all the details! When you add details, you give your audience many more reasons to be interested in looking at your drawing.

LOOK at the finished drawing! See all the different colors. When you add color your characters will really come to life. You don't have to color everything. Part of the interest in this drawing is the plain white dress, which contrasts with all the colorful details around it.

The key to creating a magical fantasy is to take different characters and place them together in an action scene.

Take a couple of your favorite characters from this book and arrange them together in an action scene. Draw them overlapping. Add lots of details.

Shade and color your magical fantasy!

Draw Magical Fantasies   **61**

Castle By The Sea

So many fairy tale stories involve castles and palaces. This castle is on a seaside shore where there is access to it by land and by sea. It is a combination of medieval castle and Arabian palace.

1   Sketch rectangles and lines to begin buildings and towers.

2   LOOK at this drawing! See the different shapes? Starting at the top, sketch the towers, turrets, windows, doors, and rooftops you see. Sketch rectangular shapes to begin the rocks on the sea side of the castle.

3   Starting at the top, Draw more windows and arches.

Draw two zigzag lines for the pathway leading up to the castle. Sketch triangles, at the bottom, left side to begin a jagged rock.

4 LOOK carefully at the final
   drawing! Can you see the
   difference in shading between the
   three sections?

   Section A shows basic shapes
   sketched lightly with some
   shading.

   Section B adds depth with more
   shading and details.

   Section C introduces even more
   shading and more details.

ARTIST'S TIP:

Drawing buildings at different levels in a drawing,
instead of placing them in a straight line, will add
depth and visual interest.

Learn about other books in
this series online at
www.drawbooks.com!